Elbows off the table

To my two young friends, Jamie Crowe and Katinka Lynch, for their invaluable help in ensuring this book covered all the areas important to young people today.

CONTENTS

This edition published in 2015 by New Holland Publishers Pty Ltd
London • Sydney • Auckland

Unit 009, The Chandlery 50 Westminster Bridge Road London SE1 7QY U
1/66 Gibbes Street Chatswood NSW 2067 Australia
218 Lake Road Northcote Auckland New Zealand

www.newhollandpublishers.com

A record of this book is held at the British Library and the National Library
of Australia.

ISBN 9781742576657

Managing Director: Fiona Schultz
Project Editor: Holly Willsher
Designer: Peter Guo
Production Director: Olga Dementiev
Printer: Toppan Leefung Printing Ltd. (China)

10 9 8 7 6 5 4 3 2 1

Keep up with New Holland Publishers on Facebook
www.facebook.com/NewHollandPublishers

Elbows off the Table

A guide to good manners and practical advice
for parents and children

Patsy Rowe
best selling author and etiquette expert

NEW
HOLLAND

school are achievements to be proud of—but not if the teachers and coaches find you rude and arrogant and your classmates dislike you. Remembering to be a caring and thoughtful person will take you a long way.

FOREWORD

*To mothers, teachers, grandmothers, indulgent
aunts and godmothers*

This book for 7–12-year-olds is the book I've always
dreamed of writing because I believe that having
good personal skills is the magic key to opening
many doors throughout life.

I'm passionate about helping young people
to be the best they can be. We all understand the
importance of doing well academically at school,
but it's equally important to balance that with
having good personal skills. An important part of
this is being well mannered—having consideration
for others and respect for their opinions, feelings,
religion and culture.

'Knowledge is power' means that when we know
what to do and how to do it we're confident and self-
assured and we manage to make others around us feel
the same way. We need to interact with others in our
day-to-day lives; how well we do it determines our
success socially, even from the earliest age. Being the
smartest person in the class or the best athlete in the

Manners Are Important

'Who needs manners?' I hear some people ask. There's a very simple answer to that: everyone needs manners! Manners are a kind of magic. They're the simple little tricks and tips that make people think, 'What a nice boy' or 'Isn't she a sweet girl?' Good manners make you pleasant and fun to have around. Having good manners also means knowing what to do, when to do it and, more importantly, how to do it, at all times. For this reason, manners also make you feel more confident about yourself, because you'll know how to stay cool in any situation. Best of all, manners are a way of helping convince others to help you and to do nice things for you—and you don't even need a magic wand!

Treat others as you would like to be treated

Whether we like it or not, other people judge us by the way we look, the way we speak and the way we behave. If our manners are good, people usually like us, but if

1

we're rude they think badly of us. Even if someone is really nice, if they don't have good manners their niceness may not come across. The other fabulous thing about being well mannered is that it makes the people around you feel good about themselves too, because you make them feel comfortable. People behave towards you the way you behave towards them, so what you give out is what you get back.

PASSWORDS TO POPULARITY: SAYING 'PLEASE' AND 'THANK YOU'

Of course, you don't have to be an expert in politeness to be popular, but you do have to know, and use, the basics. Being polite is actually very easy once you know how. The words below are the most useful words in your magic box of good manners. They are passwords to getting you out of tricky situations or to putting you in people's good books, and they pack a powerful, but polite, punch!

PLEASE ...

Along with 'thank you', 'please' is perhaps the most powerful word in the dictionary! You use it whenever you want someone to do something for you. You'll find that the best way to get what you want is just to ask nicely. When your mother asks, 'What's the magic word?' she means 'please' and it really is magic! 'Please' can make people do what you want them to do, without them even realising they're under your polite spell. That's what gives this one small word its superpowers.

You can add 'please' to just about anything and it will work its tricks. For instance, 'Could you pass the butter, please?' or 'Can I please leave the classroom?', 'Would you please come with me to the skate park?' or 'Please, Mum, can I get tuck shop today?' or 'Jayden's music is too loud, can you please tell him to turn it down, Dad'. 'Please' is also used to respond to questions or whenever something is offered to you. For instance: 'Would you like some more cake?' 'Yes, please. It's yummy, Grandma.' (Giving praise, when it's true, also helps you get your own way, but don't tell your parents I told you this! Shhhhh, it's magic!)

THANK YOU …
The other power word is actually two words, 'thank you'. People love to be thanked when they help you

out. Being thanked makes them feel special and, best of all, it makes them want to help you again, which is great news for you! You should say 'thank you' whenever someone does something kind for you. You should definitely thank someone if they have cooked you a meal or bought you a treat such as a cold drink or an ice-cream, or lent you a DVD to watch. And even if you don't like or want what they are offering, you still need to say thank you anyway. Just say it like this: 'No, thank you'.

EXCUSE ME ...

'Excuse me' is a polite phrase that gets you out of trouble. It is a very useful password because even if what you've done is a little rude, saying 'excuse me' can help smooth it over. 'Excuse me' can be used in lots of ways. Use it if you need to:

- interrupt someone's conversation: 'Excuse me, Dad. Uncle John's on the telephone for you.' Ask directions: 'Excuse me, is this the stop for the school bus?'
- pass someone who's hogging all the space on the escalator: 'Excuse me, can I get past, please?'

- attract your teacher's attention: 'Excuse me Miss Smith, what page did you say we were on?'
- apologise for bumping into someone: 'Whoops, excuse me.'

And 'excuse me' will get you out of the most trouble of all—burping, coughing, yawning, sneezing or accidentally 'bottom burping'. Saying 'Excuse me' lets people know that you weren't deliberately being rude.

I BEG YOUR PARDON ...
Using 'I beg your pardon' is the polite way to ask 'What?' You use it, or simply 'Pardon?', when you didn't hear what someone said to you. Sometimes you might hear your grandparents say, 'I beg your pardon!' if they see or hear you do something rude (which, of course, won't happen any more now that you know the power passwords!). When they say it like this, they are not asking for you to repeat the rude thing you did, instead, they're asking you to apologise, usually with a quick, 'Excuse me, Grandma, I didn't mean to burp at the dinner table'.

I'M SORRY …

Just like 'excuse me', 'I'm sorry' can get you out of almost any sticky situation, but you have to really mean it. People can see right through an 'I'm sorry' that isn't really true. Part of being a good friend, a good son or daughter, or a good sister or brother, is accepting that sometimes you may do something to upset someone and you may have to say 'Sorry'. If you forget to ring a friend for their birthday, say 'I'm sorry'. If you arrive late for class, say to the teacher 'I'm sorry Miss Smith'. You can also say 'I'm sorry' when you hear some upsetting news. For instance, when someone tells you their dog has died, you might say, 'Oh, I'm sorry to hear that'.

YOU'RE WELCOME …

Saying 'You're welcome' is really a way of saying, 'I'm so polite, I wouldn't dream of not being this way!' It's used when someone thanks you for something. For example, you may have very politely held the door open for someone and they might say, 'Thank you'. You would then respond, 'You're welcome'. Some people also say, 'Don't mention it'. Saying 'You're welcome' is a way of suggesting that it makes you happy to do something nice for someone else.

First impressions ... do you see what I see?

Now that you know your passwords to popularity, you can easily make a great first impression when you meet a stranger. Did you know it only takes 15 seconds for a stranger to decide if you are polite and nice, or rude and not so nice?

Worse, you never get a second chance to change the stranger's mind about you. If you don't make a good impression to begin with, it could be because other people don't always see you as you see yourself. If you blow it by looking at your feet and mumbling, people might think you're rude and they won't want to bother with you. Even if you're shy, try to show you are confident, this will make all the difference with first impressions. If you're sitting down when someone new is introduced to you, stand up, smile confidently, look the other person in the eye then put out your right hand and say, 'Hi, my name is Jack' or 'Hello, nice to meet you, Mrs Johnson'. If you've been invited to a friend's house for a meal and they're introducing you to their mother, say something like, 'Hello, Mrs Johnson. Thanks for having me over for lunch'.

First impressions are lasting

HOW TO GREET AND INTRODUCE PEOPLE

SECRET HANDSHAKES ...

It's polite to shake hands whether you're a girl or a boy. There is really no great mystery to shaking hands—unless you're in a secret society or something! Shaking hands connects you to the other person, and adults are very impressed when young people shake hands properly. It's good practice, too, for later in life because adults shake hands all the time, both in social situations and for business.

Sometimes you might go to shake hands but the other person doesn't want to. Don't think that just because someone doesn't shake your hand they're being rude. In some cultures males and females who are not related to each other are not allowed to touch, so it might be considered rude to shake hands. In other countries, handshaking might not be the custom. If you offer your hand and someone doesn't take it, just let it drop and ignore it. If you know you have sweaty or dirty hands, so you're embarrassed to shake for that reason, just say, 'I'm sorry, I've just been playing basketball, so I'm a bit sweaty', or 'Sorry, I've just been painting, I'll just go and wash my hands.'

Here are the only secrets you need to know to shake hands like an adult.

- Even if you're left-handed, you still use your right hand to shake hands. Put your hand out towards the other person's right hand and smile. It takes just 17 muscles to smile, but 43 muscles to frown, so smiling is a lot easier! Take the other person's hand flat, palm-to-palm, and hold it firmly. Don't just grasp or squeeze their fingers. In fact, don't squeeze or grasp at all. The idea is not to shake too hard or too limply. Don't twist or tickle or high-five or try anything fancy. Just shake the person's hand firmly but gently for about three to five seconds, while you say, 'Hello' or 'Pleased to meet you', and then let it go.

- When you're being introduced and are shaking hands, pay attention to the person's name. If you repeat their name, for instance 'Hello Pete', or 'Hi Susan', it will help you to remember their name later on. Also, don't be embarrassed to ask someone to say their name again if you didn't quite hear it. I've always preferred to repeat my name rather than being called Pansy all night instead of Patsy, which actually happened to me once!

Usually the person introducing you will say something like, 'Sam, this is my cousin, Peter'. Straightaway this gives you a clue as to how you might be able to make conversation with Peter. You might say, 'So Peter, did you grow up living close to Mike?'

How to introduce people like a pro

It can be very embarrassing for everyone if you mumble or stumble through introductions or don't bother to introduce your friends to others. When people arrive at a party, they may not spot anyone they know right away, which might make them feel a bit shy and awkward. Talking to strangers can be hard work, so it's important that you include others by giving good introductions. Make sure you say your friends' names clearly, especially if they're unusual ones.

Try saying, 'Mandy, this is Susan from my ballet class'. That way, Mandy knows who Susan is and might be able to ask her a question about ballet. You might also add (to Susan), 'Mandy used to come to ballet last year, but she's playing clarinet in the school band this year instead.' (Now Susan also has two things to talk to Mandy about—the clarinet or the school band). Giving people a little information about each other when you introduce them is a great idea, because it means that if you have to go and introduce some other people, they can continue the conversation all by themselves.

LOOK INTO MY EYES ... MAKING EYE CONTACT

Whenever you're introducing people or even talking to them, try to look them in the eye, no matter how shy you feel. If you shuffle and stare down at your feet, or look over their shoulder, it looks as if you're not interested in them or what they're saying. You also get a better idea of how the person is reacting to what you're saying if you look at their face. If they're scowling, perhaps you've made them angry, or if they are yawning, perhaps you're boring them. Looking at a person's face helps you to know what they're feeling.

YOU'RE NOT A MIND READER: ASK PEOPLE WHAT THEY PREFER TO BE CALLED

You're well on your way to being a manners magician, but remember you're not a mind reader, and neither are your friends. You might not always know how someone wants to be introduced. When you're introducing a person, you usually don't have to give their last name, unless you're introducing an adult or someone whose first name you don't use yourself, for instance, 'This is Mr Pitt, my art teacher'. Some adults are happy for children to call them by their first name. Others prefer to be addressed by their last name. Some adults might even expect you to call them Sir or Madam. It's best to start by introducing adults by their last name and then they'll tell you if they want to be called something else.

Also, don't leave your friends to guess what they should call your mum, dad or grandparents. If you're introducing your friends to your grandmother, don't say, 'Pamela, this is my grandma'. Your friend can't say, 'Hello, Grandma. Nice to meet you' because she's not *her* grandma! In this instance, you should use your gran's last name. Say something like, 'Pamela, this is my grandma, Mrs Peterson. Grandma this is Pamela, who goes to Girl Guides with me.' Your grandmother might then say to Pamela, 'Oh, you can call me Josie. I don't mind'. But it's up to the adult to decide what the young person can call them.

Most married women like to be called 'Mrs', but unmarried women might prefer to be called 'Ms' than 'Miss' these days. If you're unsure what to call a person, it is fine to ask, 'Would you like me to call you Ms White or Miss White?'—this gives her a chance to say, 'Oh no, just call me

Amanda'. In fact, whether you're at home or out, once you know what a person prefers to be called, try to use the person's name when you're speaking to them or about them. For instance, don't use 'she' if you're talking about your sister, aunt or next-door neighbour, use their name so people know exactly who you're talking about. Grandparents should be referred to as 'Grandma Ruth' or 'Grandpa Jones', doing this makes it clear which set of grandparents you're speaking about.

THE INVISIBLE GUEST: FORGETTING TO INTRODUCE PEOPLE

Nobody likes to feel invisible. When someone forgets to introduce you, it can feel a little bit as if you're invisible! But don't worry, it happens all the time and it's usually because whoever is meant to be introducing you is embarrassed that they've forgotten your name. In this case, just use your magic manners and introduce yourself, putting forward your hand and saying, 'Hi, I'm Dan. I'm in the same class as Jeff at school'. Abracadabra! No more awkward silence.

'I may as well not be here, 'cos no one can see me.'

If you're the one introducing people and you've forgotten someone's name, just 'fess up'. This is one situation where using 'I'm sorry' will make any embarrassment vanish in the blink of an eye.

Getting to Know People

Conjuring up conversations

Moving to a new neighbourhood or to a new school can be difficult. Not only are you missing your 'besties' and your old hang outs, but it can be difficult to make new friends. How do you make conversation with people you're not even sure you'll like? The most important thing is that you try. Drag out your bag of magic tricks and remember that the most important trick of all is confidence. Even if you're feeling nervous on the inside, showing confidence on the outside will make people think, 'Gee, he must know something I don't. I'd like to learn what his secret is!' Being confident doesn't mean being loud or boastful, it just means being willing to approach others and talk to them, instead of hanging back waiting for them to come and talk to you.

17

If you take the bus to school, ask someone from your class if you can sit with them. Just say, 'Excuse me, can I sit here?' or 'Excuse me, is this seat taken?' If they're listening to their MP3 player, they may not be in the mood to talk, but if they're reading a book you can try asking, 'Good book?' Their response will let you know whether they're interested in a conversation. If they just say, 'Yeah', and continue reading, you shouldn't interrupt them again. But if they say something like, 'Yeah, but not as good as the last one', you can then ask, 'Who's the author?' or 'What's it about?' or 'I haven't read *Twilight* yet'— you might find they're happy to chat.

If someone is just gazing out the window, you could try saying something like: 'Hi, I've seen you in my computer class. They have heaps better computers at this school than at my old school'. One of the most important things to remember about being a good conversationalist is that you also need to be a good listener. Part of listening is also 'hearing' what the other person's body language is telling you. If you conjure up a conversation and the person keeps giving you short answers and looking out the window, they would probably prefer not to chat. But if they respond and start to ask you a few questions too, or give you long answers that reveal more about themselves, then go ahead and keep chatting.

Try conjuring up conversation with the following topics:

- ask what classes or subjects they take;

- ask which teachers they like or don't like;

- ask about school sports or activities. For example, 'Are you in the football team?' or 'I wouldn't mind joining the school band, do you play any instruments?'

- tell them about a great new movie you've seen recently, or a computer game you like to play;

- you might ask them what music they like, and even offer to swap songs or let them listen to a new band on your iPod;

- you might ask them about the new neighbourhood. For instance, 'What do you do on weekends around here?', 'Where is the best skate park?' or 'Wow, I love your skateboard. Where did you get it?'

Don't ask question after question after question, otherwise the other person will feel they're being interrogated and not charmed. Instead, stop and wait for them to answer and, hopefully, ask their own questions. You don't need to be a magician to see when someone has had enough.

COMPLIMENTS ... HOW TO GIVE AND RECEIVE THEM

When someone says something nice to you, it's called paying you a compliment. We all like to hear nice things about ourselves, but some people get embarrassed when being complimented because they don't want to seem full of themselves. To accept a compliment, all you have to do is smile and say, 'Thank you.' If they say, 'Wow, you look really nice wearing a dress. You should wear dresses more often', don't brush them off with, 'I hate dresses. Mum said I had to wear one today.' Not accepting the other person's compliment will make them feel uncomfortable. They meant to make you feel good about yourself by saying how nice you looked, so don't make them feel bad.

Compliments can be a good ice breaker, too. For instance, if someone you just met says to you: 'I love your sneakers. Did you buy them here?' it gives you the chance to say, 'No. I bought them when we went on holiday to Hawaii last year. They're much cheaper in Hawaii. Have you ever been there?' Even if they haven't, they might respond by telling you where they went for their last holiday, saying something like, 'No, but we went skiing last year and it was really cool.' Or if there is an awkward silence you might ask them, 'Where does your family like to go on vacation.' Sometimes the simplest things can be great conversation starters.

DON'T BE TOO CLEVER ... USE NICE LANGUAGE

Confidence is about being cool, calm and collected, not about being clever or being a smart alec. Trying to be too popular too quickly can just get you into trouble. Using four letter words, or expressions like 'cool bananas', or speaking like a 'gangster ho' might make you look foolish instead of cool, especially if you're speaking to someone who doesn't talk like that. You might think it's grown-up to swear because the first time you hear swearing is usually from grown-ups. It doesn't make you grown-up though. Anyone can swear, so why be like everyone else? Using swear words all the time is very boring (and sometimes embarrassing) for anyone unlucky enough to be listening to you. Rude or hurtful remarks like 'get lost', 'dry up', 'shut up', 'get stuffed', 'you suck' and 'loser' certainly won't help you make or keep friends. It's better to impress people with the power of your personality, rather than trying to bewitch them with bad language.

TRANSFORMING YOURSELF INTO A NICER PERSON

It's sometimes hard to make new friends, and if you're shy it's even harder. But you can learn to draw others to you with the power of your personality. Not everyone who is popular is nice, but being nice is a really good way to be popular.

- Be friendly, say 'Hi' and 'Bye' and ask others about their day, week or life.

- Include other people. Ask kids sitting on their own at lunch time to join your group—you never know, they may be fascinating once you start talking to them, they might even invite you over to play X-box or swim in their pool. Most importantly, treat others as you would like them to treat you. Welcome new people to your school or sports club by showing them where the toilet block is, directing them to the woodwork room, or telling them what time training starts. (Remember how alone you felt when you changed schools.)

- Don't talk about people behind their backs; you wouldn't like it if they said things about you.

- Don't pass on rumours. It might not be true, and it might 'snowball' into something that could really damage someone's reputation and cost them friends.

- It's great to make new friends, but don't push aside an old friend to hang out with someone new and cool. Old friends know the real you, and there's room in your life for both old friends and new friends.

- All magicians know how important it is to keep their secrets safe. If someone tells you a secret, it's because they think you're special and trustworthy enough to keep it. Don't prove them wrong by blabbing it to everybody.

- Offer to help people, whether someone is struggling with their homework or has a chore to do when you visit. Being popular is all about being a nice person and helping others when you can.

- Respect and return the things you borrow, before your friend has to ask you for them back.

- Don't be boastful of your achievements. Others will be far more impressed if they hear you've been made school captain from your friends than from you.

- If you hear that a friend's parents have separated or divorced, don't spread the news and don't try to make a sad situation funny by cracking a joke. Let them mention it if they want to, and tell them you're there to talk to if they need you.

I WISH THEY'D DISAPPEAR!
BE POLITE EVEN WHEN OTHERS ARE IRRITATING YOU

Everyone knows someone who they'd rather not hang out with. Try not to be that person. No one likes people who interrupt conversations all the time, tell corny jokes, are boring, whinging, gossipy, too talkative, or brag about how much pocket money they get. Sometimes we wish people like that would just disappear!

Don't be impatient (well at least don't show it) when someone else is speaking, and certainly don't interrupt them in mid-sentence. It's rude to finish someone else's sentences for them because you think you can guess what they're going to say.

Even if someone asks you a dumb question (or the same question they asked you before) you still need to answer it politely, although you can say, 'Sorry, I thought I told you this morning I couldn't go swimming tomorrow'. Perhaps they didn't hear you the first time.

NOW, LISTEN VERY CAREFULLY ... THE ART OF LISTENING

People who are self-absorbed are usually very poor listeners, and no one wants to bother talking if they're not going to be heard. Sometimes people can bore us (let's hope we don't do the same thing) but it's hurtful to show that you're not interested, so wait until there is a pause in the conversation and then introduce another subject or another person to the conversation. Before you plan your escape, you could try to get them off the topic and onto another one. Try changing the subject using, 'Did you know that...?' If that doesn't work, just say, 'Hey, I've got to go. I've got heaps of homework due for tomorrow. See you later okay?' and vanish before they start talking again!

TEASING AND BULLYING ...

Being a dobber won't win you any friends either. Nor will contradicting people all the time or being a show-off or know-it-all. It's great to have a good sense of humour, but not when it's always at someone else's expense. Imagine how you'd feel if everyone was always making fun of you. It's much cleverer to be a magician than a clown. There's a fine line between harmless teasing and straight-out bullying. Teasing can get out of hand if it goes on for too long or if there are too many teasers, even if it is something rather harmless, like making jokes about a bad haircut.

*Don't tease people who are different,
instead make them a friend.*

Watch people's reactions carefully. If the person being teased starts to look uncomfortable, frustrated, annoyed and isn't joining in and having a laugh, let the joke drop. It's not funny any more. Some topics should be left alone altogether. Remarks about weight, personal attacks, or saying sexist things like 'You throw like a girl' are just plain rude. If someone has bad breath, dirty hair or pimples, or wears daggy clothes, don't mention it; if you do, you'll make them feel awful and embarrassed, and that's the last thing you want to do. Trying to palm off what you've said by adding, 'Just kidding', doesn't work. It's too late. Even if in your own mind you're teasing in a fun way, remember that words can be hurtful and ganging-up on people is cruel. Also, don't say anything over the internet or by text that you wouldn't say face to face. Bullying is still bullying no matter how it is done.

LEARN TO 'AGREE TO DISAGREE'

There are lots of times in life when we don't agree with what someone says. Rather than saying, 'That's dumb', 'You've got to be kidding', or worse, 'Come off it, I don't believe you', try just saying 'Really?' or 'Isn't that interesting? I've never thought of it that way.' If someone keeps going on and on about it, you can say, 'Whatever?' and let it go or just say, 'OK, I'm going to go and watch a DVD'. If you're sure they're wrong, you can try to put your point across gently, but the secret is to recognise when they're not going to budge anyway. There's not a lot in life that is really worth arguing about, so even if you do strongly disagree with something 'agree to disagree' and move on.

WINNERS AND LOSERS ... BEING A GOOD SPORT

It's great when you or your team wins, but it's very important to also be a good loser. Congratulate your opponents. You wouldn't like it if you had just won something and then your opponent 'talked down' your win. So if you lose, lose graciously. Certainly don't whinge or whine if you lose, it makes you look like a sore loser. Even during the match, saying bad things about the other team only makes you look mean, so try to be positive towards them and say, 'Nice goal' if you believe it was. People always admire a good loser and a modest, non-boastful winner.

Be a modest, not a boastful winner.

Being a Good Host

Getting in on the act...
Inviting friends over

So you've succeeded in making friends and keeping them, now it's time to really wow them by getting them in on your act. When your friends are on your turf, that's when you can really impress them, so you may want to ask them around to your house. It's okay to text, email or telephone your friends to invite them over, but make sure you're clear about what will be happening and when. Don't put out a 'blanket' invitation on Facebook or on a school noticeboard or community noticeboard of any type. It spells trouble with a capital T.

Make it clear whether you're asking your friends over for dinner, to watch a DVD or play a game, for a sleepover, or just to come and hang out for a few hours after school. Perhaps you're asking them over because it is your birthday or you're having an end-of-term party or a Halloween party. If that's the case and there's something special you want them to come to, then you'll need to tell them what to wear. There's nothing more embarrassing than turning up in jeans and sneakers at a fancy dress party, or worse, turning up in fancy dress when everyone else is in jeans and sneakers. If you're having a pool party, you'll need to remind them to bring swimmers. You don't want

'Only four people said they were coming!'

them to feel left out so tell them when it starts, and when it ends.

THE IMPORTANCE OF THE RSVP

Unless you have a crystal ball, you'll need to know how much food to ask your mum and dad to buy. Try to do as much as you can to help them prepare everything, as it's your party. Sending a proper invitation, even by email, and asking for an RSVP (this is an abbreviation for *repondez s'il vous plait*, which is French for 'Please Reply') means your mum doesn't have to be a fortune teller about how many people will need to be fed. If you want them to reply by phone or by email, tell them, and give your telephone number or email address. And make sure to include a date by which they must let you know whether they are coming or not. While we're talking about replying to invitations, if you get an invitation, you should reply as soon as you can. That's only polite and it means the host will know how many to cater for. Even if you can't go, let them know straightaway so they can ask someone else in your place.

WHAT DO YOU DO IF 20 PEOPLE RSVP'D AND ONLY FIVE ARRIVE?

Whenever anyone has a party, they hope everyone they've invited will come. It's very disappointing (and really very rude) if only five people turn up, especially if you and your parents have bought and prepared enough food for twenty guests! But there's no point letting your other guests see your disappointment—otherwise you'll all have a miserable time. Step into another room for a minute and send out a quick text message, or ring around to ask why some of them haven't turned up. It may be that they're late or that they've forgotten. If you can't contact them, forget them. It's your party, go and weave your magic on your other guests and have the best time you can have. Next time, you might like to ring around the day before to make sure it doesn't happen again!

WHOOPS, YOU'VE FORGOTTEN TO RSVP

If you suddenly realise that a party you've been invited to is on this weekend, but you haven't yet replied, phone right away. Say you're sorry not to have replied and ask if it's still okay to come? But be prepared to be told that you can't. If you can't, apologise again and promise to reply sooner next time.

THE HOST WITH THE MOST

When your friends come to your house, you're the host, so you need to show them where to put their coats, bags or any other gear they've brought, and to make them feel welcome. Introduce them to your parents or step-parents, and to any other friends you've asked over. If it's a big group, make sure no one is left out because they're too shy to include themselves. The first thing to do is to offer your guests something to eat and drink. If there are a lot of kids coming, it can be a good idea to ask some of your most confident and outgoing friends to help you out as hosts. They can keep an eye on the shy kids, make sure people have food and drinks, and tell everyone where the bathroom is.

SHARING IS CARING ...

When you were a toddler, your parents most likely taught you to 'play nice'. Sharing shows that you're thinking of others as much as yourself. If you invite someone to your house and you're playing games like X-box, don't forget to share the controller with your guest, after all you want your friends to enjoy themselves too and not just be an audience for you. Letting your friend go first will make them feel special—after all, it's your game and you can play it whenever you like. It's the same when it comes to sharing food and drink. Let your friend have the last sausage roll or the biggest slice of chocolate cake; you can have the biggest piece when you're the visitor in their house.

'Boy, this game is really cool.'

What's in the box? Unwrapping gifts

If it's your birthday and unless you've told people otherwise, they'll probably bring presents. But should you open them as soon as people arrive, or wait until later? Well, that depends on the size of the party. If you have any more than four guests, it's not a great idea to start opening gifts when each guest arrives. It distracts you from your role as host and it means you might overlook introductions or not get your guests a drink. If you have a lot of guests, you might like to have a table or a bed where all the gifts are placed until you can open them. If a present doesn't have a card with it, you might need an 'assistant' to write the person's name on the outside of the gift, so that when you open it you know who to thank. Later on, after you've cut the cake and had your fun, you can open your presents all at once. Remember to thank all of your guests equally. Don't be really excited about your new 'SingStar' game but be half-hearted about the pair of socks your nanna has knitted for you. Also, even if someone has given you something you already have, create the illusion that you're happy with the present. After all, they've taken the trouble to buy you a gift.

WHAT CAN YOU DO WITH A GIFT YOU DON'T LIKE, DON'T WANT AND HAVE NO USE FOR?

If you know your friend well enough and don't think they'll be hurt, you could ask where they bought it and would they mind if you exchanged it. You could swap it for something your brother, sister, cousin or best friend has that you want. Or rewrap it and give it away to someone else later, but make sure you don't give it back to the person who gave it to you!

If it's something you can't give away, keep it in a cupboard and when your friend visits, put it out. It's a bit sneaky, but if it makes them happy, it's worth doing. Remember, they *thought* you'd like it.

WHAT DO YOU DO IF GATECRASHERS ARRIVE AT YOUR PARTY?

Ask a parent or older person to deal with uninvited guests known as 'gate crashers', but be ready to call the police if there are a lot of them or they are clearly a gang. If your party is going to be a big one, it might be a good idea to ask some of your friends' parents to come along anyway, in case something like this does happen.

Being the Best Guest

If you're not the host but a guest, then your role is to fit in as well as possible and make it a pleasure for your host to have you in their home. For the most part, it means being easygoing and treating their house and their family even better than you treat your own.

To be the best guest, you should:

- do your best to fit in and go along with whatever activities have been planned. Remember, you may have a mum, a dad, a sister and Rover the dog, but not everyone has the same family situation. Some families have step-parents, some may be single-parent families and your friend might be an only child. Other friends might be adopted or live with their grandparents. Whatever the case, don't ask personal questions like, 'Why does your dad live in the shed?' If they want you to know about their family situation, they'll tell you in their own good time, but putting them on the spot just causes embarrassment.

- be polite to all the family, including pets. Don't tease the dog, cat or budgie.

- remember not to go to the refrigerator to help yourself to food or drink—ask.

- try not to wander around the house picking up ornaments, looking at everything, or prowling around—it looks as if you're being nosy.

- if you need to use the telephone, ask.

- wait for everyone else to start eating before you tuck in. The family may say a blessing before eating the meal. So just sit quietly with your head bowed and watch to see what everyone does.

- carry your plate to the sink at the end of the meal and offer to help with the washing up or stacking the dishwasher, even if they say 'Don't bother'.

- say 'Thank you' for the meal. If you enjoyed it, tell them so. If you didn't, still say, 'Thank you for dinner'.

- remember to say 'Bye. Thanks for having me' when you leave.

Other families might have different customs from your own.

'When in Rome, do as the Roman's do' is a saying that means you should try to make yourself blend in. Other families might have different home customs to you, for instance they might eat with chopsticks, or sit on the floor to eat, rather than at a table. They might not eat meat. Men and women might eat separately and your friend's parents might sleep in separate bedrooms. Their mother might wear a headscarf. It is not your place to comment, stare or make them feel unusual. Remember that, in their home, you're the one who's unusual. Even after you have left their house, don't make remarks about how your friend's family lives or the weird or eccentric things they do. Good guests don't blab.

HOUDINI SITUATIONS:
GETTING OUT OF STICKY MOMENTS

Sometimes when you're staying at a friend's place, you might find yourself in a situation you really would like to get out of. Perhaps your friends' parents have had a huge argument and everyone is sulking, or perhaps they've had bad news and everyone is very upset. In these situations, it's okay to suggest that you ring your parents and have them come and pick you up. However, sometimes it might be only something small and you need to know how to wave your magic wand and disappear into the backyard or into your friend's bedroom and leave the grown-ups in private.

WHAT TO DO IF ...

you accidentally spill your drink on the carpet or break a glass. Admit to it and say you're sorry. Do what you can to clean up the mess and offer to replace the glass. They probably won't accept your offer unless you've broken something really special to them, but they'll feel pleased that you offered.

you feel homesick. Ask if you can use the telephone to call your parents. You might find that once you speak to them you'll feel much better. If you still want to go home, it's okay to ask your parents to come and get you, depending on how far away you live and what time of the day or night it is. Phoning your parents when they're at work or in the middle of the night will just upset everyone.

you have an argument with your friend. First, try

to apologise or smooth things over. You obviously like each other or you wouldn't have accepted their invitation in the first place. If it can't be sorted out you might suggest that you go home, depending on where you live and what time it is. Going home is really a last resort. A manners magician will usually find a way to solve the problem.

you have an allergy to cats, dogs or birds and you can feel an attack coming on. Tell your friend's parents straightaway. If you have your inhaler or your medication with you, you should take it and try to play in another room or outside away from the source of your allergy. If you've forgotten your medication, or you start to feel worse, ask your friend to ring your parents—after all, you may need to see a doctor or go to hospital and your parents need to know.

your friend's family has received bad news. If you're a good friend, it might be that you can help by answering the phone, making cups of tea, or just trying to comfort your friend and keep them company. But if everyone is really upset, you can

Tabletop Tricks ...
How to Use Cutlery

Knowing how to behave at the dining table, whether you're visiting a friend or eating out at a restaurant, is a great confidence builder. When you're out at a restaurant, or when you've been invited for a formal dinner at a friend's place, you might find much more cutlery is laid out than at home, which could be very confusing. So you'll need these magic tricks up your sleeve to use the cutlery correctly.

'Whoa, what's with all the knives and forks?
Is an army coming to dinner?'

First, don't comment on the way the table is laid out. For instance, don't say, 'Whoa, what's with all the knives and forks? Is an army coming to dinner?' This just makes it obvious that you don't know what you're doing. Second, if you're really stuck for which glass to use or which knife to pick up first, the best thing to do is to watch what your host (or the person who invited you out to dinner) does and copy them. Don't be too obvious when you copy them so it looks like you're a copycat, just wait and see what they do and then do the same thing as if it's what you do all the time!

Dining dos for terrific table manners

As a rule of thumb, you should do the following things in this order:

1. Take your cap or hat off at the table, or your 'hoodie' if you're wearing one. Also take off headphones or earphones, and put your mobile on silent or better still, turn it off altogether. You can clear any messages later. Never take or make a phone call during a meal, and that goes for texting too.

2. Unfold the napkin and place it in your lap. Don't tuck it into your belt or the neck of your shirt. Napkins only ever get tucked in to your neckline if you're eating something very messy, like seafood or spaghetti bolognaise.

3. Only start to eat once everyone has been served, or once your host tells you to. Your friend's family might say a prayer or say a blessing or grace before they eat, so you need to sit quietly and wait until everyone is ready before you start.

4. Use cutlery from the outside, in. It can be pretty overwhelming when you're faced with a lot of cutlery. The golden rule is to start from the outside and work inwards so the outside knife matches the outside fork.

Here's the breakdown:

- *On the right side of the plate* you'll find the soup spoon and a knife. Your water glass will also be on the right. An easy way to remember it is that anything that is liquid, like soup or drinks, will be to the right of your plate.

- *On the left side of your plate* will be a fork and your small bread plate, where your bread roll will be placed. Usually, the only knife on your left is the one you use for your bread or bread roll and butter and it can rest on your bread and butter plate. This small butter knife is sometimes already on the plate when you sit down.

- *Don't swap your knife and fork*, unless you're left-handed or you're eating something like rice or pasta and need to use just your fork. And when you've finished eating, put the knife and fork back in position, as if you were right-handed.

5. Pass the salt and pepper, butter, sauce, gravy, platter of food, or the water jug to others when they ask. And if you need anything passed to you, ask the person nearest to you to pass it.

6. Make polite table conversation throughout the meal (but don't talk when your mouth is full). There are plenty of topics that are fine to discuss at the dinner table. You can talk about pretty much the same things you might say when you are trying to get to know someone new—your family, sports, movies, television, news or holidays. Try to pick something that you think they will find interesting and watch to see how they're reacting. Are they looking at you and listening carefully? Are they interested and asking questions? Or are they sliding off their seats with boredom? If they are, quickly get off the topic by asking them a question. If someone asks you a question just after you've taken a bite of food, just put your hand over your mouth apologetically and continue chewing, then swallow the mouthful and say, 'I'm sorry ...' and continue the conversation normally.

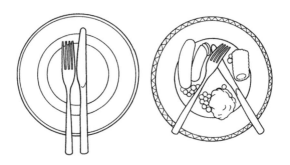

7. Place your knife and fork side by side, facing the 12 o'clock position on your plate once you've finished. If you're out in a restaurant, the 12 o'clock position is especially important as this is the magic sign that lets the waiter or waitress know that you've finished your meal and they can take your plate away. If you've not quite finished but are just having a break for a minute or two, place your knife and fork upside down on your plate and leave them in a v-position.

8. Remember to thank the host when you finish and to say how much you enjoyed the meal.

DINING DON'TS ...

- Don't put your elbows on the table.

- Don't hold your knife and fork pointing
  straight upwards or wield them like medieval
  swords and tridents. Don't wave your knife and
  fork around in the air—you're not conducting
  an orchestra! Also, don't pretend your knife is
  a chainsaw and that broccoli is a tree. In fact,
  don't play with your cutlery or with your food.
  Pick your knife and fork up only when you
  need to use them.

- Don't hold your knife like a pen.

- Never lick your knife (or your plate).

- Don't turn your fork over and use it like a
  shovel, unless you're eating one of the tricky
  foods like curry, risotto or spaghetti.

- If it's a help-yourself buffet or all-you-can-eat
  meal, don't overload your plate as if you haven't
  eaten all week. If you want more, you can go
  back later.

Don't gobble and guzzle.

- Don't slather your food with salt, pepper or butter before you've tasted it. It's very rude as it means you think the food your friend's mum or dad has cooked might be tasteless.

- Don't chew with your mouth open.

- Don't talk with your mouth full.

- Don't mop up gravy or sauce using your bread roll. (You can at home though!)

- Don't gnaw at bones. If it's a small bone, like a chicken wing or a delicious drumstick, you may pick it up in your left hand and chew it, but without making loud crunching or gnashing noises.

- Don't lean across the table to grab salt, pepper or more food or drink; instead ask the person who is closest to it to pass it to you.

- Don't say 'Yuk!' if you see something on your plate that you don't like (or don't recognise.)

- Don't gobble your food. You need to pace yourself so you're not the first one to finish, but don't dawdle either or make everyone wait for you to finish eating before they can have dessert.

- Don't push your plate away when you finish eating.

GREAT ESCAPES ... ALLERGIES OR OTHER PROBLEMS

Here are some great escapes to get you out of any dodgy dining situations.

What if I'm allergic to some foods? If you're being invited to someone's home for a meal and you're allergic to certain foods, always tell them that when you accept the invitation, so they don't serve it to you. If they forget and give you something you can't eat, just remind them that you're allergic to it and leave it on the side of your plate. If you're highly allergic to it and it can't even be on the same plate, you might have to just fill up on bread rolls. Usually, if you tell someone you're very allergic to the food they've served, they will fix you something else. It's unlikely you'll starve!

What do I say if someone gives me food I've never tried before ... and I don't like the look of it? Take a little bite, but if it tastes as bad as you thought it would, shuffle it around the plate and hide it under something else. If someone notices, just say, 'Sorry, I'm not that fond of brussel sprouts'.

What do I do if I see a creepy crawly in my salad?
There's no need to make a fuss and draw attention to yourself (or to the bug) if you're at a friend's place. Instead, just lift it out and put it on the edge of your plate. If it's a *big* creepy crawly, you might like to ask to be excused and take your plate to the kitchen where you can pitch it into the sink without anyone seeing. If it is really gross like a dead fly, a maggot or a squashed bug that might ruin the meal for you, you might have to just pretend you've had enough if you're at a friend's place. If you're out at a restaurant, you can politely signal to the waiter and say, 'Excuse me, there's a dead fly in this soup, can I have another bowl, please?'

What do I do if I need to leave the table? Just say, 'Excuse me for a minute' and place your napkin on the table to the left side of your plate (if there's room) otherwise just put it on your chair.

TIPS FOR TACKLING TRICKY FOOD

Soup. When you're eating soup, don't slurp it or tilt up the bowl and pour it into your mouth. The right way to do it is to take your spoon and do a shallow scoop from the front or middle of the plate towards the back, then sip up the soup from the spoon as you place it in your mouth. This way, if it splashes it doesn't splash on you (and the soup cools while you draw it away and back towards your mouth).

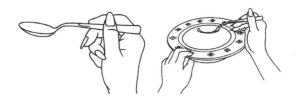

Bread rolls. Take just one bread roll and one butter pat (or miniature butter packet) and place it on your bread and butter plate (the small round plate to the left of your fork). Before you start to eat a bread roll, the first thing you need to know is that you shouldn't ever cut it in half with your knife. Instead, you should carefully (so that crumbs don't spray all over the tablecloth) break off a bite-sized piece of the roll, butter just that piece, and eat it. Once you've eaten that piece of roll, break off another small piece, butter it and eat it. The idea is that your bread plate shouldn't look like a demolition area!

Corn on the cob. There are two ways you can eat corn on the cob. The first is to hold the corncob at each end with the little prongs that most restaurants serve it with, and bite into it. (If there aren't any prongs, just use your fingers to hold the cob either end.) This can get pretty messy, so you need to ask for a paper napkin if your host hasn't given you one, as you might be wearing a lot of the melted butter on your face otherwise. The second way is to hold the corncob in your left hand, (or hold it firmly with your fork) and then, using your knife, slice off the kernels from top to bottom down the cob so the kernels fall onto your plate. Then you can eat the kernels with your fork held in your right hand.

Pasta. Noodles and pasta can be slippery suckers to eat. For that reason, pasta is one of the few meals where you're allowed to hold the fork in your right hand. If you're at a restaurant, they may give you a spoon as well as a fork.

Hold the spoon in your left hand and twirl your fork a few times with spaghetti on it around the bowl of the spoon. Don't hold the spoon up in mid-air as pasta will drop off on either you or the tablecloth! If there's no spoon, you take the fork in your right hand and select a few strands of spaghetti and twist them into a neat little coil on the end of your fork. It's much easier if you keep the fork down on the plate while you twist.

Manners on the Move, Being Polite in Public

Your manners magic is not just on display when you eat at a friend's place or at a restaurant, but also whenever you're in public. People will always judge you on the way you behave. Whether you're on a bus, a train, or at a public event, manners are needed more than ever.

Be prepared: take a tissue

Alright, so it's the motto of the Boy Scouts rather than the manners magician, but it's true that sometimes when you're out in public, you may be the one who gets surprised by a sticky (or a snotty!) situation you hadn't expected. Always carry a pack of tissues with you in your bag, and grab one as soon as you feel you might sneeze. Turn away from the people around you, then sneeze gently into the tissue. Don't draw attention to yourself by doing a big 'Ahhhh-chooo!'

If it's the first of a series of sneezes, just say, 'Excuse me' and move out of the room. It's the same with coughing—cover your mouth with your hand or with a tissue and try to cough as quietly as you can. If you have to spit afterwards, try to do so without too much throat rattling and then throw the tissue away if possible. When it comes to burping or any other bodily noises you might make, if you're sure someone heard you, say 'Excuse me'. If they're polite, they won't comment either.

Open sesame! Opening doors

It's polite to open a door then to stand back and let older people walk through before you, and it's also polite to hold it open for the person behind you. It shows that you respect older people and that you're thoughtful of others. When someone opens a door for you, or holds it for you, remember to say, 'Thank you'. It's also polite to push the 'open door' button on an elevator if you've seen someone walking towards the elevator as the door begins to close. If you go somewhere where they have revolving doors, just pause and wait until the 'door' revolves your way, then step in and walk. Don't push the door so it goes faster.

SIT-DOWN MANNERS ... GIVING UP YOUR SEAT

Remember that whenever you're on a bus, train or aeroplane, you're sharing that space (and those seats) with others. Don't be selfish and put your bag on the seat beside you, unless the bus or train has lots of empty seats. Your backpack should be placed under the seat, where no one can trip on it.

No one likes sitting on something smeared on the seat, so keep your feet on the floor and chewing gum in your mouth. At the movies too, your feet should be on the floor, and not on the back of the seat in front of you.

On buses and trains ...

- Stand back and let people get off the bus or train before you get on.

- Help older people or pregnant women if they have bags or parcels.

- Give up your seat on the bus or train for someone older than you or someone who is frail (perhaps with a walking stick), a pregnant woman, or a mother with young children in tow.

- Don't block the passageway with backpacks or bags.

- Don't put your feet on the seats.

- Don't kick the seat in front of you.

- Don't eat or drink if it's not permitted.

- Don't point or stare or make remarks like, 'Why is that woman in a wheelchair?' or 'What happened to that man's leg?'

- Don't play your MP3 player or iPod so loudly that the other passengers are forced to listen to your music blaring out of your headphones.

- Don't talk at the top of your voice on your mobile phone.

STAND-UP MANNERS ... WHEN TO STAND

- Stand up for elderly people, pregnant women, women with small children or anyone who has a limp or is using a walker or a cane.

- You need to stand up whenever you're being introduced to someone older or when someone new enters the room.

- You may also need to stand up in church during parts of the service (just stand up when everyone else does).

- You need to stand up when the national anthem is played at a concert or sporting event (unless it's on the TV).

- You need to stand up at a funeral or parade or service when everyone else stands up.

- You need to stand up at a wedding when the bride enters the church.

- You need to stand up when an important person, such as the prime minister or the governor-general, enters the room.

- You need to stand up if you're at someone's place for dinner and their grandma or grandfather arrives. It's a sign of respect because they're an older person.

- Standing up to be introduced is very important as not only is it rude to stay sitting down when people are meeting you but it's very awkward reaching up to shake hands.

Special Occasions

Wedding manners

Weddings are happy occasions and lots of fun, but they're also a lot of work to organise. Just imagine if you had to arrange a dinner for hundreds of guests and make speeches in front of all your friends and relatives. You'd probably be a little stressed. So if you have a relative who is getting married, don't add to their wedding hassles by going on and on about not being asked to be a bridesmaid, a groomsman, an usher, a flower girl or whatever. If you are invited to be part of the wedding party, try to fit in as best you can. It's the bride and groom's big day, not yours, so don't complain if you don't like the dress or you think wearing a bow tie is uncool.

If you're not used to going to a church, synagogue, mosque or temple, ask your mum and dad what you can expect. Above all else, remember that these places are places of worship and are usually

67

very formal, so you need to be quiet and respectful. When you arrive, don't yell out to people you know, run up and down the aisle, or fiddle with the flowers. Just sit down quietly and wait for the bride to arrive, then stand up when everyone else does. And, of course, turn your mobile phone off, and don't even THINK about texting!

NO LAUGHING MATTER ... FUNERAL MANNERS

Weddings may be joyful occasions, but funerals are terribly sad ones, and you need to be able to keep it all together when someone you know has died. There is no magic you can weave to lessen the pain of losing a loved one, the only thing you can do is try to be as helpful and respectful as possible. No one wants to lose someone they love, but the grief is made even worse if your family is worried about how you might act at the funeral. If you go to a service at a funeral parlour, mosque, synagogue or church, watch what other people do and do the same. Be quiet and respectful, but remember that it's okay and perfectly natural to be sad, to cry, or to need a hug at a funeral. Take tissues with you, so you can wipe your face and nose and can offer them to others. A lot of people are likely to be upset and crying, so don't feel that it's embarrassing. If you don't need to cry, don't stare or point at anyone else who is crying.

People sometimes feel so bad at funerals that they try to 'lighten up' the situation by cracking a few jokes or telling loud silly stories about the person who has passed away. This is not very clever because it may seem as if the person doesn't care and it may upset other people there. It's always hard to know what to say at funerals and even adults don't always get it right, so if you find you do need to say something to someone who is very upset, just say 'I'm so sorry about Uncle Ted', and leave it at that.

Sometimes at a funeral, the body of the person who has died is placed in an open coffin to be 'viewed' by the family and friends. This can either be at the church or place of worship where the service is being held—or at the home of the deceased person. Viewing the dead person is not seen as gross, it's seen as the chance to say a final goodbye, but it can be upsetting to see someone you loved like this. If you would rather

everyone is up, so you can all open your presents together—and the suspense makes it even more fun.

RECEIVING CHRISTMAS GIFTS ...
So Nanna didn't get you the Bratz doll you asked for ... well, don't complain, moan or show your disappointment. If you didn't get what you hoped for, especially with grandparents' gifts, it may be because they forgot what you wanted, didn't have the money or didn't think the gift you wanted was appropriate. They may even have bought your present much earlier in the year. Above all else, use your magic tricks—put on a happy face and look pleased with your gift. There's no need to make them miserable even if you're disappointed.

And if you have guests, don't abandon them to play with your new presents. Even if you're stoked with your new MP3 player, digital camera, or laptop, don't disappear into your bedroom in a puff of smoke and ignore everyone else for the rest of the day. After all, your relatives and friends came to your house, or you went to theirs, to be together, not to just exchange gifts then ignore each other.

Psssst ... and now for another trick that will truly enchant your relatives. Your mother, father, grandparents and aunts and uncles have probably been busy for days getting ready for Christmas Day, and it will amaze them if you offer to help out by serving drinks and taking food to the table, carrying dirty plates to the sink and stacking the dishwasher. You can charm just about any adult with a little bit of elbow grease.

THANK-YOU NOTES

Accepting gifts graciously doesn't just apply to those that are given to you in person. If someone from out of town sends you a gift for Christmas or for your birthday, you should thank them by writing them a thank-you note or card of some kind—just a few lines or you can thank them by email, Facebook, Skype, or even by text. You need to let them know you've received their gift and tell them how much you like it (even if you don't). If a grandparent, aunt or uncle, or godparent has sent you a gift and then doesn't hear from you, they may wonder whether you received it at all, or they may feel hurt that they went to the trouble of buying something for you and you haven't bothered to get in touch and say thanks.

If you've been taken on holiday by a friend's parents or have stayed a few days with them, it's also nice to take the time to write and send a thank you. You don't have to write a lot; in fact, you can even buy a 'Thank You' card and just add your name at the bottom.

The best thank-yous, however, are personal.

For example:

Dear Aunty Patsy

Thank you for the money you sent me for Christmas. I'm saving up for a bike and this will really help.

I'm looking forward to seeing you next Easter and you'll be able to see my new bike then I hope.

Love
Harry

How easy is that?

MOBILE PHONE MANNERS

If you do decide to ring to thank someone for a gift, make sure your mobile phone wizardry is as good as your manners in person. There's no doubt that mobile phones are wonderful inventions. Being able to call or text your parents, relatives and friends whenever you like is a great way to stay in touch, but mobiles can be a real nuisance if we just use them willy-nilly without thinking of others.

Often people think that because it is slightly hard to hear someone on a mobile phone, they need to shout into the phone to be heard. That is not the case, and other people on the train, bus, or in the library or doctor's waiting room certainly don't want to hear all the personal details of your life. Just because your mobile allows you to be mobile, doesn't mean all conversations are suitable for all places. So respect other people's personal space—and be aware that telling the world about your private life makes you look like a show-off.

Mobile dos and don'ts ...

Always turn off your phone or put it on silent if you're at a friend's home for a meal, at a movie, at a concert, at a wedding or funeral (or in any place of worship), in a restaurant, in a library, or anywhere a sign instructs you that mobiles are not to be used.

Don't talk on your phone in a public toilet—no one wants to hear you on the toilet.

Don't have a long conversation with someone on the phone and neglect the people you're with. Excuse yourself and tell the caller that you're not free to talk and you'll call back later, and then get off the phone quickly before your friends feel as if they're being ignored.

The same thing applies with texting. It's very rude to spend time texting other friends and ignoring the friends you're with. Save texting other friends until you're on your own.

If your phone has a camera, don't think it's funny to take photos of your friends in awkward situations. It can land you in a lot of trouble if the photos fall into the wrong hands and could really embarrass your friends or get them into trouble.

If your parents pay for your calls, make sure you know what your monthly call limit is and stick to it.

There really is no need to shout. If you or the person you're calling is in a loud place or can't hear, call back later.

PHONE RULES FOR LANDLINE LUBBERS ...

Your parents might already have rules about how they like you to answer the phone at home, especially if someone works from home, but if they don't, then a good way is to pick up the phone and say, 'Hello,' and say the telephone number. Never give out your first name to someone you don't know over the phone as it could be dangerous if someone you don't know calls and asks questions, say you're sorry you can't talk and hang up. It might be an innocent call, but it might not be, so don't give out any information to people you don't know.

If someone you don't know asks, 'Is your mum or dad home?' don't let them know you're home alone if both of your parents are out. It's best to say, 'Dad's in the shower right now, can I take a message and have him call you back? This is sometimes how thieves find out if someone is home or not if they are thinking of breaking into your house.

Don't give information to callers you don't know

Keep a notepad and pencil beside the phone so you can write down a message if you need to.

No smoke signals please ... how to take messages

Being able to take a good phone message is very important, after all, you'd hate to miss out on some great news because someone forgot to tell you. Good message-taking skills are also very handy if you want to get a part-time job when you're older. Parents get extremely annoyed to be told, 'Oh, Mum, someone called for you,' —Who called? What's their phone number? A good message should include this information. You wouldn't want to get a message like, 'Grace, some boy rang for you. His name was John or Jeff or something. He said he'd ring back.'

If the caller wants to speak to someone else in the house, don't yell out, 'Hey Julie, someone's on the phone'. Get the caller's name, cover the mouthpiece and say, 'Julie, John Fuller is on the phone for you'. If you don't know where Julie is, just say, 'Can you hang on a minute, while I see where Julie is?' Then go and find her without yelling out her name as you go around the house.

MAKING A CALL ...

When you're calling someone, always say your name: 'Hello, this is Josh. Is Britney there, please?' If you have a popular name like Jack, Tom or John, make sure you say your last name as well so they know which John, Tom or Jack you are.

Try to be considerate with other people's time. Don't call during meal times, early in the morning or late at night, and find out interstate or overseas time differences before you ring people. Remember there could be a sleeping baby in the house, or in some families the parents might work shift work and go to bed early, so it's a good idea to ask, 'Is it okay to talk now?'

If you have 'Call Waiting' and a call comes through when you're already having a conversation, excuse yourself for a few seconds but no longer, and tell the second caller you're already on a call and you'll phone them back. Then return to the first caller. It is extremely rude to get caught up in a second call and keep your first caller waiting for you to return, or to keep swapping between two callers.

PICK A NUMBER, ANY NUMBER ... DEALING WITH
WRONG NUMBERS

If you think that someone has dialled the wrong number, just say, 'Sorry, I think you have the wrong number'. Don't just hang up in their ear right away. If they ask what your phone number is, don't answer instead ask, 'What number were you trying to ring?' or 'What number do you want?' and then, when it doesn't match your number, say, 'Sorry that's not this number'. If it is your number, then you can say, 'Well, that's our number, but there's no one here by that name, sorry'.

If you're calling a friend and you ask, 'Could I speak to Jane, please?' and the person who answers says, 'There's no one called Jane living here', say, 'I'm sorry, I must have dialled the wrong number. I'm trying to call 5577 8895'. If the other person says, 'That's not this number' you should say, 'Sorry, my mistake' before you hang up.

The same goes for telemarketers. Simply tell them, 'Sorry but we're not interested', and hang up quickly before they get into their stride. There's no need to be rude, everyone has to make a living somehow and they're just doing their job.

And finally, don't stay on the phone all night so no one else can use it!

Netiquette

Some commonsense rules …

Nowadays you're probably more likely to spend more time on the internet than on the telephone, but similar rules apply. The net is great for finding information, helping with homework and staying in touch with friends, but you shouldn't say or do anything online that you wouldn't say or do in person.

Just as it's unsafe to give out personal details (or those of your friends) to any phone caller you don't know, don't give out private information in an email or online. Chatting with someone online doesn't mean you know them—they could be anyone. By personal information, I mean your name, your address (or even your suburb), your telephone number, your mobile phone number, your date of birth, your parents' names, what school you go to, or where you go after school. Also, don't give that information out in chat rooms and limit the amount of information about yourself that you put on Facebook, My Space and Twitter or any other online forum or social networking site. Be very careful what information you give about other people. You might think nothing of writing that your sister is pregnant and her boyfriend has just dumped her, or that your brother has failed his driver's licence for the third time, but these are private matters to stay within the family. You don't know how someone might 'use' this information to embarrass them or hurt them—or you—so be careful what you reveal.

Your password is also precious. Make sure your parents know it, but aside from them, don't tell anyone what it is, not even your closest friend. If your password falls into the wrong hands, it could be dangerous.

If someone you've chatted with online suggests you meet in person, tell your parents and discuss it with them. Never meet anyone you have met online on your own. If your parents think a person seems genuine, one of your parents may choose to go with you to meet the person in a public place, like a coffee shop or a shopping mall. Remember, you never know who might be on the other side of the computer.

'SEND' SORCERY ... EMAIL ETIQUETTE

I'm the first person to admit that emailing is excellent. It's fantastic how easy it makes staying in touch with friends and exchanging files and photos, all done with a click of the 'send' button. But, emails come with their own set of problems, the first of which is that it is easy to take an email the wrong way.

Before you hit 'send', think for a couple of seconds about what you want to say and the tone you want to say it in, especially if it's a touchy subject, like asking someone to return something they've borrowed—or telling them you're not coming to their party after all. Think about how the person will feel when they read your email. When a person reads an email, they don't have the advantage of seeing the sender's face, so they can't see if you're smiling or not (unless you include an emoticon like a smiley face). They also can't hear the tone of your voice to understand that you're not upset or angry. They can only go on what you've written.

Even if you're really mad, don't let that come across in an email. Don't use capital letters, which, in emails is like shouting. In fact, it's better not to write an email at all when you're angry; wait until you calm down. Certainly you should never threaten or bully people in an email—or anywhere for that matter. Remember, words can really hurt. Jokes that might be laughed off in person can wound when they're read over and over again, or forwarded on to others. Remember too that it's easy to misunderstand an email, it might not mean what you think it means, or what the sender intended it to mean, so word emails carefully.

If you're receiving hurtful or threatening emails you should tell someone you trust: a school counsellor, an older brother or sister or your parents. Don't reply to the emails or forward them to anyone! If you ignore them, the person sending them won't be sure you're even getting them and it's not much fun sending nasty emails if you don't get a reply. Remember, the person is doing this to hurt you, so if they don't know if they're upsetting you, they will probably give up.

Foolish forwarding

That's another thing ... remember that anyone you email can simply hit 'forward' and send your email on to anyone else. Anything you write can be circulated to dozens or hundreds of people—throughout the world, within seconds. So if you're being nasty about someone, it may well fall into their hands, and once you've written it, it can't be taken back. If your email is passed around in cyberspace, it might end up being very embarrassing for you and you might even lose friends. It can affect your school life, or your parents' jobs, or mean you have to move to avoid the embarrassing fallout. Don't write anything online and think that it's private—it isn't.

When you write an email, write it as you would a letter or essay. Use the spell check—you don't want to look lazy or ignorant—and write complete sentences without using abbreviations like, 'I feel Gr8. U?' Don't just launch into your message, but start with 'Hi' or 'Hello' and sign off with 'Bye' or 'See you tomorrow'. Remember that the briefer the message the more chance there is of it sounding curt or harsh.

BEING PROPER WITH YOUR 'PROPS': HATS, SHOES & BAGS

Every magician has all sorts of props that help them with their act. Your must-have items are probably much more normal than a magician's might be—phone, hat, schoolbag, shoes and skateboard—but it still helps to know how to use them considerately if you want to enchant parents, teachers and your friends' parents.

HATS OFF TO YOU ... WHEN TO TAKE YOUR HAT OFF

Wearing a hat is a must, especially in very hot countries, but remember that how you wear certain pieces of clothing can influence how people judge you. Taking off your hat is a sign of respect in some instances. You should take your hat or cap off when you're being introduced to an elderly person—or when you go to someone's home. It's also considered very rude to wear a hat at the theatre or in a restaurant, in fact in many indoor places.

BAREFOOT BANDIT ...
REMOVING SHOES
When you go to some places, like some Japanese restaurants, or to a home that has carefully polished floors, you may have to take your shoes off. If you see shoes at the front door, ask if you should take your shoes off, and if so, remove them. Hopefully your feet won't be too stinky.

BACKPACK BASICS
If you carry a backpack, don't just throw it by the entrance when you get home—or when you visit a friend's place. Ask where you should put it. Backpacks can take up a lot of space, so when in public, don't put your backpack on the seat and don't leave it lying around or you'll start a security scare. If you're wearing a backpack, be very careful when you walk up a supermarket aisle or in any small space like a train or an aeroplane—you don't want to send objects flying or knock out the person behind you when you turn around.

Skate sensibly

Pavements are for people to walk on, so if you ride a skateboard or a bicycle, ride it only in areas where it is allowed. Slow down if you see someone walking in front of you. If you're coming up behind someone walking, and especially someone with small children, call out, 'Excuse me' to warn them, then go wide around them. Don't endanger others, or yourself, by trying to be cool and skidding along pavements or down handrails. No one else wants to have to clean up your blood, or their own, from the pavement.

Planetary politeness ... don't litter

Manners help you be considerate to others around you, but it's not just people you need to think of, it's also plants, animals and the planet itself. It is definitely not cool to litter—it's just irresponsible and lazy. Pitch your rubbish into a bin (or, even better, in a recycle bin if it is recyclable) and encourage your friends and family to do the same. After all, we all want to live in a beautiful, clean and healthy environment.

BEING POPULAR FOR LIFE

Remember, friends are precious. Don't just contact friends when you want something, because no one likes to feel they're being used. It's not always easy to make friends, so don't lose touch with the people you've liked in the past. If you've been a good friend and other kids have enjoyed hanging out with you, they won't want to lose touch with you either. Having good manners will make you a nice person to be around, so friends and adults alike will want to experience a little bit of your bewitching charm.

Remember, being well-mannered is easy. It's all about:

- treating other people as you'd like them to treat you;

- respecting others' thoughts and opinions, their religion and way of life, and, above all, their differences; and,

- using your pleasant personality to make others feel good and get what you want the nice way.

If you can remember these, then you'll enjoy manners magic for life.

Other books by Patsy Rowe

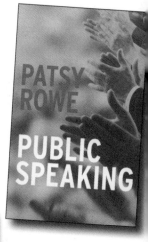

www.etiquette.com.au

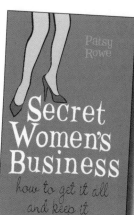

BUSINESS ETIQUETTE

REVISED AND UPDATED 3rd EDITION

Keep your competitive edge and maintain successful business networks

• job interviews • email etiquette
• social media • networking
• events & conferences • public speaking
• international etiquette

PATSY ROWE

Patsy
Rowe

Secret Women's Business

how to get it all
and keep it

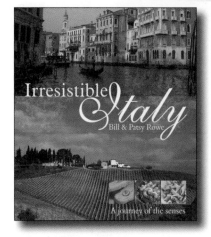

Irresistible Italy
Bill & Patsy Rowe

A journey of the senses

AM I HAVING FUN YET?

PATSY ROWE

More riotous fun from the bestselling author of
NO SWEAT NOT TO WORRY SHE'LL BE JAKE

YOU *ARE* LEAVING TUESDAY AREN'T YOU?

PATSY ROWE

More riotous fun from the bestselling author of
NO SWEAT NOT TO WORRY SHE'LL BE JAKE
and **AM I HAVING FUN YET?**

NO SWEAT NOT TO WORRY SHE'LL BE JAKE

PATSY ROWE

Over 16000 copies sold